SHILOH

National Military Park, Tennessee

by Albert Dillahunty

NATIONAL PARK SERVICE HISTORICAL HANDBOOK SERIES NO. 10
WASHINGTON 25, D. C. 1955   (Reprint 1961)

The National Park System, of which Shiloh National Military Park is a unit, is dedicated to conserving the scenic, scientific, and historic heritage of the United States for the benefit and inspiration of its people.

SHILOH

National Military Park - Tennessee

By Albert Dillahunty

All rights reserved, which include the right to reproduce this book or portions thereof in any form except provided by U.S. Copyright Laws.

Digital Scanning and Publishing is a leader in the electronic republication of historical books and documents. We publish many of our titles as eBooks, paperback and hardcover editions. DSI is committed to bringing many traditional and well-known books back to life, retaining the look and feel of the original work.

Trade Paperback ISBN: 1-58218-781-9

©2010 DSI Digital Reproduction
First DSI Printing: June 2010

Published by Digital Scanning Inc. Scituate, MA 02066 781-545-2100 http://www.Digitalscanning.com and http://www.PDFLibrary.com

Contents

	Page
PRELIMINARY CAMPAIGN	2
THE FIRST DAY	9
THE SECOND DAY	16
RESULTS OF THE BATTLE	19
GUIDE TO THE AREA	24
Iowa State Monument	24
Michigan State Monument	27
Confederate Monument	27
Ruggles' Batteries	28
Confederate Burial Trench	28
Illinois State Monument	29
Shiloh Church Site	29
Fraley Field	30
Putnam Stump	30
Hornets' Nest and Sunken Road	31
Johnston's Monument	31
Peach Orchard	32
War Cabin	32
Bloody Pond	33
Indian Mounds	33
Overlook	33
Pittsburg Landing	34
NATIONAL CEMETERY	35
HOW TO REACH THE PARK	35
ADMINISTRATION	36
RELATED AREAS	36
VISITOR FACILITIES	37
SHILOH INSPIRES WRITERS	37

Shiloh Church, painted by Capt. A. M. Connett, 24th Indiana Volunteer Infantry, a participant in the battle.

SHILOH NATIONAL MILITARY PARK preserves the scene of the first great battle in the West of the War Between the States. In this 2-day battle, April 6 and 7, 1862, both the Union and Confederate Armies suffered heavy casualties, bringing home the horrors of war to the North and South alike. Nearly 24,000 were killed, wounded, or reported missing—a number equal to more than one-fifth of the combined Union and Confederate Armies engaged in the battle. By their failure to destroy the Federal Armies at Shiloh the Confederates were forced to return to Corinth, Miss., relinquishing all hold upon West Tennessee, except a few forts on the Mississippi which were soon to be wrested from them. Their failure at Shiloh foreshadowed the loss of the Memphis and Charleston Railroad, the South's vital line of communication between Chattanooga and the Mississippi. After the fall of Memphis, early in June, the Federals were in position to strike at Vicksburg, the conquest of which would give them control of the Mississippi and split the Confederacy in two.

The psychological effect on the South of the Union campaigns was probably of greater importance than the material gains or losses of the contending armies. The Confederates learned by bitter experience the error of their former opinion of the Union soldier. No longer could they boast that the fighting ability of one Confederate was equal to that of 10 Federals, now that Southern dash and chivalry had been grievously tried against Northern valor and endurance.

The near-defeat at Shiloh removed the illusion of easy victory, created by the fall of Forts Henry and Donelson, from the minds of Northerners. They now realized that the struggle was to be a long and bloody one. A few days after Donelson, one Union soldier wrote: "My opinion is that this war will be closed in less than six months from this time." Shortly after Shiloh the same soldier wrote: ". . . if my life is spared I will continue in my country's service until this rebellion is put down, should it be ten years."

Shiloh is not distinguished by outstanding generalship on either side, but it is interesting as a battle fought by raw volunteers—young men without previous experience in a major engagement and with little or no military training.

Preliminary Campaign

War activity west of the Appalachian Mountains in 1861 was confined chiefly to the States of Kentucky and Missouri. Toward the end of the year when loyalty, or at least the neutrality, of the governments of these border States seemed assured, the Federals began making plans for the invasion of the South by way of the western rivers and railroads. Each side began to maneuver for strategic positions. The Confederate General, Leonidas Polk, believing that the Southern States were about to be invaded through Kentucky, moved up quickly from his position at Union City, Tenn., and seized Columbus, Ky., the northern terminus of the Mobile and Ohio Railroad. Gen. Ulysses S. Grant, recently appointed commander of the Federal troops in and around Cairo, Ill., had made preparations to occupy that important river port and railway center on the following day. Thwarted at Columbus, Grant retaliated by taking Paducah, Ky., located at the junction of the Tennessee and Ohio Rivers.

It now became apparent to the Confederate high command in Richmond that a strong line would have to be established along the northwestern border of the Confederacy before the Union armies had time to occupy more of the strategic points. They believed that the task could be performed more effectively if all troops in that theater of operation were placed under one commander. Accordingly, Confederate President Jefferson Davis sent Gen. Albert Sidney Johnston to the West with the imposing title of "General Commanding the Western Department of the Army of the Confederate States of America."

Arriving in Nashville on September 14, 1861, General Johnston studied his difficult assignment. The line he was supposed to occupy extended from the mountains of eastern Tennessee westward across the Mississippi to the Kansas boundary. Only two points on the proposed line were then in Confederate hands: Columbus, which he considered the natural key to the Confederate defense of the Mississippi, and Cumberland Gap, Ky., which he had previously ordered Gen. Felix K. Zollicoffer to occupy.

One of Johnston's first official acts upon arriving at Nashville was to order Gen. Simon B. Buckner to secure Bowling Green, Ky., one of the most important railroad centers south of the Ohio. He also ordered garrisons to the incomplete works at Fort Henry, on the Tennessee, and Fort Donelson, on the Cumberland, hoping to prevent a Union advance up either of these natural highways. A Federal offensive up the Tennessee or the Cumberland would endanger the important railroad and industrial center of Nashville, Tenn.

Since the outbreak of the war, Nashville had been converted into a huge arsenal and depot of supplies. Large quantities of food, clothing, and munitions had been collected and stored in its warehouses. Its factories were turning out percussion caps, sabers, muskets, saddles, harness, knapsacks, cannon, and rifled pieces. Its looms were turning out thou-

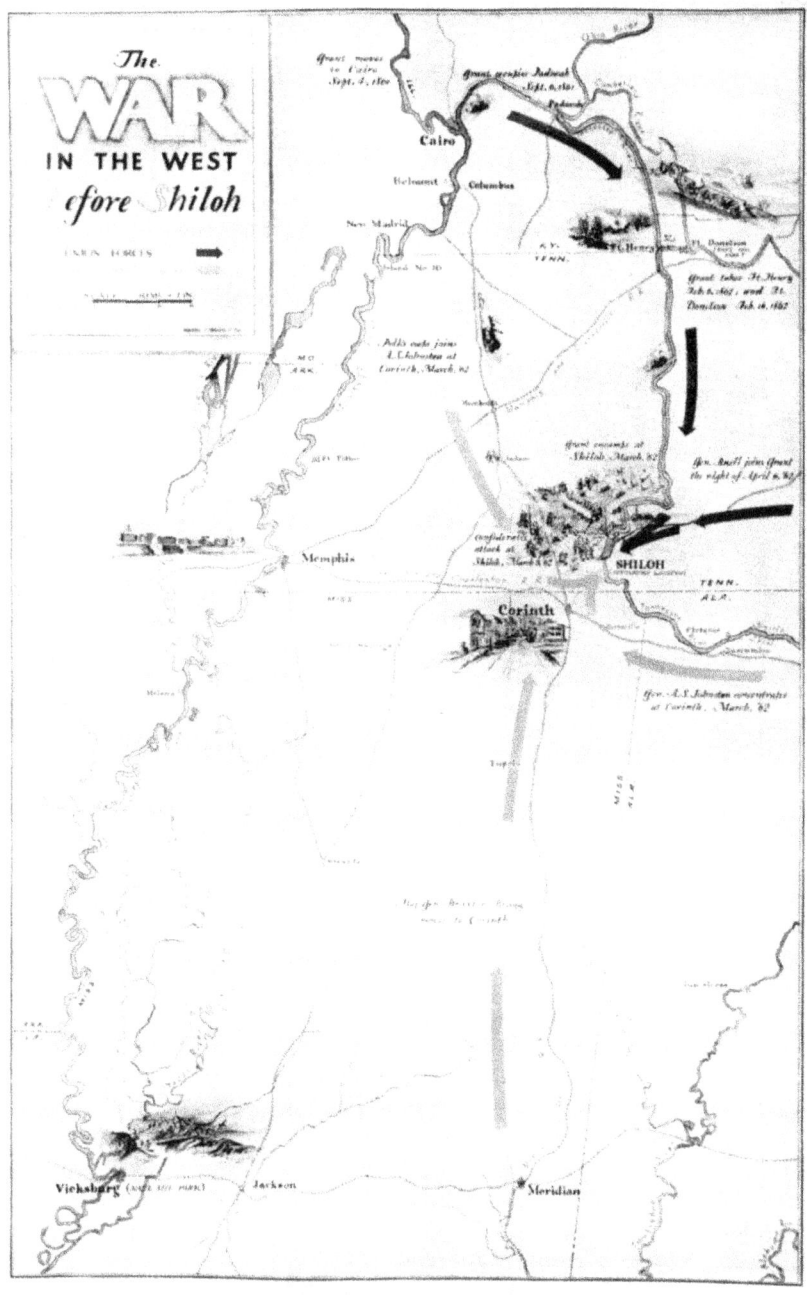

Commodore Foote's gunboats ascending the Tennessee to attack Fort Henry.

sands of yards of gray cloth which were being made into uniforms for the soldiers. The loss of this city would be an irreparable blow to the Confederacy.

While General Johnston was establishing his positions, the Federals were rapidly organizing their forces preparatory to an attack upon the Confederate line. Gen. Henry W. Halleck, from headquarters in St. Louis, was strengthening his positions at Cairo, Ill., and Paducah, Ky. At the same time, he was making ready a large number of river steamers so that his troops could be moved by water to almost any point along his front. From headquarters in Louisville, Gen. Don Carlos Buell, commander of the Department of the Ohio, reinforced his line so that Johnston had to keep his main force at Bowling Green, Ky., to guard the important railroads which penetrated Middle and West Tennessee.

Various plans for an attack upon the Confederate line were considered by the Federals. General Halleck, commander of the Department of the Missouri, believed that it would take an army of not less than 60,000 men, under one commander, to break the well-established line. He, therefore, asked that General Buell's army be transferred to him, or at least placed under his command.

Before a union of the two departments could be effected, General Grant asked for, and received, permission to attack the line at Fort Henry. A combined land and naval attack by Grant's troops and the gunboat fleet of Commodore Andrew H. Foote resulted in the surrender of Fort Henry on February 6, 1862, and the capture of Fort Donelson, with about 12,000 prisoners, on the 16th. The loss of these forts broke Johnston's line at its center and compelled him to evacuate Bowling Green and Columbus, permitting western Kentucky to fall into Union hands. To prevent encirclement, he was also forced to withdraw from Nashville, abandon Middle and West Tennessee, and seek a new line on the Memphis and Charleston Railroad.

Following the fall of Forts Henry and Donelson, Grant incurred the displeasure of General Halleck by sending a division of troops into Buell's department at Clarksville. Halleck's indignation increased when he learned that Grant had gone to Nashville for consultation with Buell. Halleck directed the withdrawal of the division from Clarksville, suspended Grant from command, and ordered him to Fort Henry to await orders.

Dover Tavern, General Buckner's headquarters and scene of the surrender of Fort Donelson.

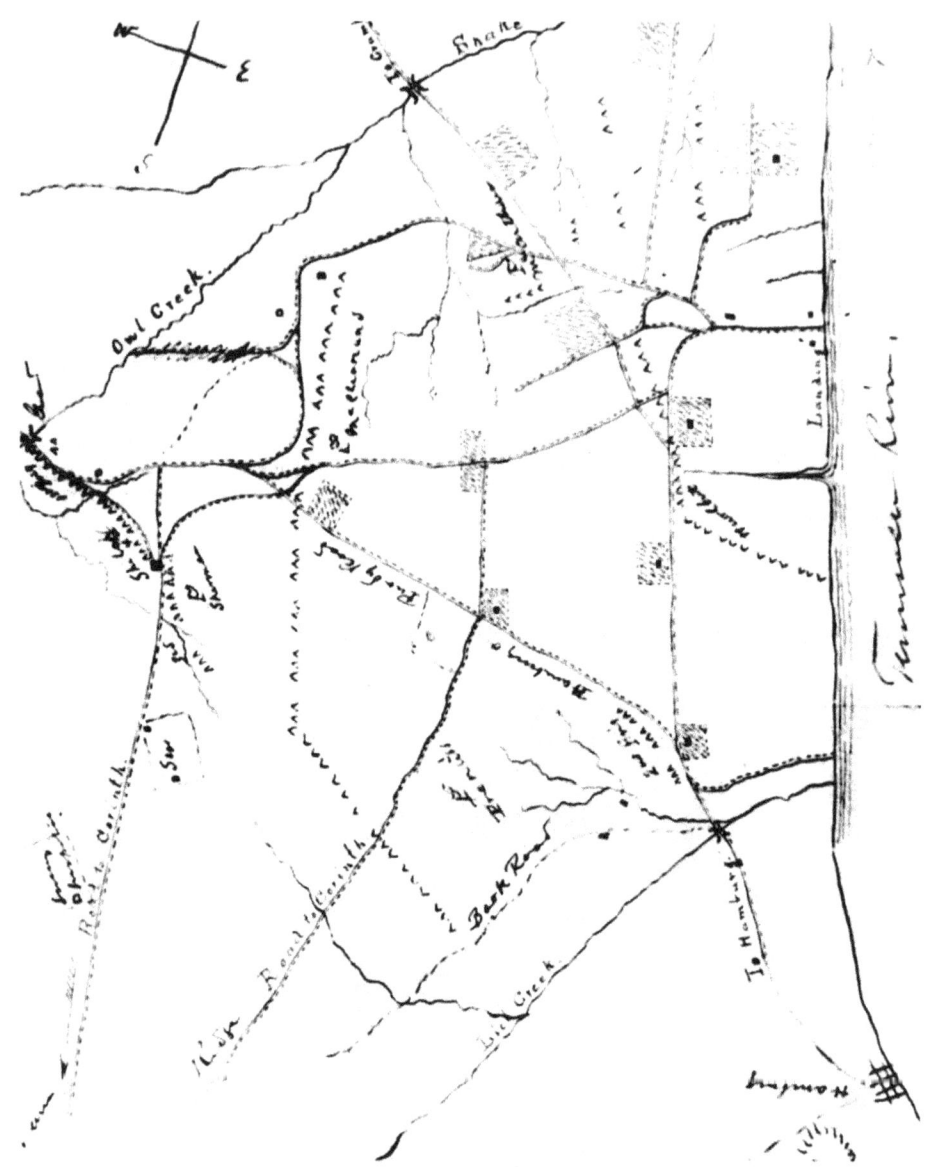

Map of the battlefield of Shiloh, made by Gen. W. T. Sherman soon after the battle.

The army under Grant's successor, Gen. Charles F. Smith, moved up the Tennessee toward the heart of the Confederacy, with the intention of rendezvousing at Savannah, Tenn., on the east side of the river. Gen. Willian T. Sherman was sent forward on the so-called Yellow Creek Expedition for the purpose of destroying railroad communications to the west of Corinth, Miss., the objective of the campaign. High water made Sherman's mission a failure, and he was compelled to return. He reported to General Smith that a more convenient place for the assembling of his army was at Pittsburg Landing, Tenn., 9 miles above Savannah, and on the west side of the river, from which direct roads led to Corinth. General Smith, therefore, instructed him to disembark his division and that of Gen. Stephen A. Hurlbut at Pittsburg Landing, in positions far enough back to afford room for the other divisions of the army to encamp near the river.

Conference of Confederate commanders the night before the battle. From left to right, Gen. P. G. T. Beauregard, Gen. Leonidas Polk (seated), Gen. John C. Breckinridge, Gen. A. S. Johnston, Gen. Braxton Bragg, and Maj. J. F. Gilmer. Gen. W. J. Hardee was not present.

Cherry Mansion, Savannah, Tenn., used as headquarters for the Union Army, March 13 to April 29, 1862. While eating breakfast in this house, General Grant heard the sounds of heavy firing which told him the battle had begun. Generals W. H. L. Wallace and C. F. Smith died here in April 1862.

In obedience to this order, Sherman encamped his division along a ridge on either side of Shiloh Church, almost 3 miles from Pittsburg Landing, with General Hurlbut's division about a mile to his rear. Within a few days, Gen. Benjamin M. Prentiss' division took position on Sherman's left, while Gen. John A. McClernand and Gen. W. H. L. Wallace formed their divisions between Sherman and the river. The 3d Division, commanded by Gen. Lew Wallace, was stationed at Crump's Landing, about 4 miles downstream from the main encampment. Thus, by April 5, 1862, there were in the five divisions of the Army of the Tennessee at Pittsburg Landing 39,830 officers and men present for duty and 7,564 at nearby Crump's Landing.

While this concentration of troops was in progress, General Smith received a leg injury which became so serious that he had to give up his command. General Grant was restored to duty and sent to Savannah with orders to concentrate troops and supplies, but to bring on no general engagement until a union could be made with Buell's army, and Halleck had arrived to assume personal command of the combined forces.

General Johnston, in the meantime, was concentrating all available forces at Corinth, Miss., on the Memphis and Charleston Railroad. After this had been accomplished, he resolved to take the offensive and attack Grant's army at Pittsburg Landing, hoping to defeat that army before it could be reinforced by General Buell. Hearing that Buell was nearing Savannah, Johnston determined to attack at once and accordingly on the 3d of April issued the order for the forward movement. He expected to give battle at daylight on April 5th, but heavy rains and bad roads made progress so slow that the last of his columns did not reach the field until late afternoon. It was then decided that the attack should be postponed until daylight the next morning. Johnston's army, 43,968 strong, went into bivouac in order of battle within less than 2 miles of the Federal camps. The Confederate forces were formed in three lines. Gen. W. J. Hardee's corps and one of Gen. Braxton Bragg's brigades were in the first line, the remainder of Bragg's corps in the second line, and Generals Leonidas Polk's and J. C. Breckinridge's corps in the third line.

During the night of April 5th the two hostile armies were encamped within a short distance of each other: the Confederates poised, ready to attack, while the unsuspecting Union army went about its normal camp routine, making no preparations for the defense of its position. On Saturday, a few hours before the battle, Sherman wrote Grant: "I have no doubt that nothing will occur to-day more than some picket firing," and that he did not "apprehend anything like an attack" on his position. The same day, after Sherman's report from the front, Grant, who was at Savannah, telegraphed Halleck: "I have scarcely the faintest idea of an attack (general one) being made upon us, but will be prepared should such a thing take place."

The First Day

The battle began about 4:55 a. m., Sunday, April 6, when a reconnoitering party of Prentiss' Union division encountered Hardee's skirmish line, under Maj. Aaron B. Hardcastle, a short distance in front of Sherman's camps. The reconnoitering party—three companies of the 25th Missouri under Maj. James E. Powell—fighting and retreating slowly toward its camps was reinforced by four companies of the 16th Wisconsin and five companies of the 21st Missouri. These troops were, in turn, reinforced at the northeast corner of Rhea Field by all of Col. Everett Peabody's brigade. Here they succeeded in holding the Confederates in check until about 8 a. m., when they fell back to Prentiss' line of camps, closely followed by the enemy.

General Sherman, hearing the picket firing in his front, immediately got his division under arms and posted a battery at Shiloh Church and another on the ridge to the south. The left of this hastily formed line

The Confederate charge upon Prentiss' camps. From "Battles and Leaders of the Civil War."

received the full impact of the Confederate onslaught at about the same time that Prentiss' camps were attacked. One of the regiments in the left brigade—the 53d Ohio—consisted of raw troops who had never been under fire. Unable to withstand the fierce Confederate attack, this regiment soon broke and fled to the rear. A short time later the other two regiments of the brigade did likewise. The commander of the brigade, Col. Jesse Hildebrand, refused to leave the field with his men. Since he had no troops of his own, he acted as aide for General McClernand the rest of the day.

General Prentiss, in the meantime, was making a gallant, but futile, stand along his line of camps. Assailed by the eager Confederates in front and on the flanks, his whole division soon broke and fell back in confusion. He succeeded in rallying about 1,000 of his men on the center of a line that W. H. L. Wallace and Hurlbut were forming with parts of their divisions in a strong position in the rear. This new line, running through a densely wooded area along an old sunken road, proved to be such a strong position that the Confederates named the place "Hornets' Nest" because of the stinging shot and shell they had to face there.

Meanwhile, General Grant at breakfast in Savannah heard the guns in the battle of Shiloh. He at once sent word to the advance of Buell's army, which had already arrived at Savannah, to march immediately to the point on the river opposite the battlefield. He then hurried up the river aboard the steamer *Tigress,* moving in close enough to the shore at Crump's Landing to instruct Gen. Lew Wallace to be prepared to execute any order he might receive. Upon arriving at the field, he dispatched reinforcements to Prentiss and formed two regiments in line near Pittsburg Landing, to arrest the tide of stragglers from the battle and organize them to return. He then rode to the front.

While the Confederate right was engaged with Prentiss, the left, supported by continuous artillery fire, was hurled against the combined forces of Sherman and McClernand who were making a stubborn stand along the ridge at Shiloh Church. This small log building, which gave its name to the battle, was considered the key position of the field, as it commanded the best road from Corinth to Pittsburg Landing. When General Grant reached the church, about 10 a. m., his troops were heavily engaged all along the line. They had resisted the relentless pounding from the Confederate artillery and the repeated infantry charges for over 2 hours. Seeing that the line could not hold much longer, Grant dispatched orders to Lew Wallace to move to the field, expecting him to reinforce the Union right. Leaving Sherman, he moved down the line to the left to confer with his other division commanders. He visited Prentiss in the Hornets' Nest and directed him to hold his position there at all hazards.

Union defenders of the Hornets' Nest (right) repulsed 11 Confederate charges against the Sunken Road.

The Sunken Road near Bloody Pond.

Soon after Grant's departure, Sherman withdrew from Shiloh Ridge, abandoning his camps and much of his equipment. He took a new position behind the Hamburg-Purdy Road alongside McClernand who had been pushed back on line with Prentiss' Hornets' Nest position.

Grant's army was now posted on either side of Prentiss, making a line approximately 3½ miles long. The opposing army was charging this line with a series of frontal attacks, just as hard on the left as on the right. This was contrary to Johnston's plan of battle. He had intended to push hardest on the Union left and seize their base of supplies at the Landing. Without supplies or an avenue of escape, he hoped to drive the disorganized Federals into the swamps of Snake and Owl Creeks and destroy them.

Seeing that the enemy was being driven into its base of supplies rather than away from it, Johnston, about noon, moved to the extreme right to direct in person the activities of that wing of his army. There, he found his troops exposed to a galling fire and unable to advance. Determined to move his line forward, Johnston ordered and led a successful charge. The Union lines recoiled, and the Confederates surged forward about three-fourths of a mile. As Johnston sat on his horse, watching the lines re-form, a ball from the gun of an unknown Union soldier struck the Southern commander, severing the large artery in his right leg. No surgeon being near, he died from loss of blood at 2:30 p. m.

The death of Johnston caused a lull in the battle on the right flank for about an hour. The situation was relieved somewhat by the fact that a second in command was on the field. Gen. Pierre G. T. Beauregard was in charge of headquarters which had been established near Shiloh Church. When informed of Johnston's death, he immediately assumed command. He sent General Bragg to the right of the field and put Gen. Daniel Ruggles in command at the center.

General Ruggles, having witnessed 11 unsuccessful charges against the Hornets' Nest, decided to concentrate artillery fire upon the position. Therefore, he collected all the artillery he could find—62 pieces—and opened fire upon the Union line. Under cover of continuous fire from these guns, the Confederates attacked with renewed courage and redoubled energy. Unable to withstand the assault, the troops on both the Federal right and left withdrew toward the Landing, leaving Prentiss and W. H. L. Wallace isolated in the Hornets' Nest. As the Union forces withdrew, the left of the Confederate line swung around and joined flanks with the troops moving around from the right, thus forming a circle of fire around Wallace and Prentiss.

Wallace, seeing that the other divisions were withdrawing and that his command was being surrounded, gave the order for his troops to fall back. To execute the order, his division had to pass through a ravine which was already under the crossfire of the encircling Confederates. Wallace was mortally wounded in the attempt, but two of his regiments succeeded in passing through the valley, between the Confederate lines, which they appropriately named "Hell's Hollow." Prentiss continued the resistance until 5:30 p. m., when he was compelled to surrender with over 2,200 troops—all that remained of the two divisions.

During the afternoon, Col. Joseph D. Webster, Grant's Chief of Artillery, placed a battery of siege guns around the crest of a hill about

Johnston mortally wounded.

Gen. Ulysses S. Grant.
Courtesy National Archives.

a quarter of a mile in from the Landing. The smaller field artillery pieces were put in position on either side of them as they were moved back from the front. The two wooden gunboats, *Tyler* and *Lexington,* anchored opposite the mouth of Dill Branch, further strengthened the line. As the remnants of the shattered Union Army drifted back toward the Landing, they were rallied along this line of cannon.

After the capture of Prentiss, an attempt was made to reorganize the Confederates for an attack upon the Union position near the Landing. Before a coordinated attack could be made, Beauregard, who had received word that Buell would not arrive in time to save Grant's army, sent out the order from his headquarters at Shiloh Church to suspend the attack. Unknown to Beauregard, the advance of Buell's army had already arrived opposite Pittsburg Landing and was being rapidly ferried across the river.

During Sunday night and Monday morning, Buell moved approximately 17,000 troops into line on the Union left. Lew Wallace put al-

Gen. Don Carlos Buell.
Courtesy National Archives.

most 6,000 fresh troops—Fort Donelson veterans—in position on the right. The Confederates, receiving no reinforcements, spent a sleepless night in the captured Union camps annoyed by shells from the gunboats, which were thrown among them at 15-minute intervals throughout the night.

The battle had already raged for 13 hours. Charge after charge had been made by the Confederates, followed by Federal countercharges. Ground had been gained and lost, but the general direction of movement had always been toward the Landing. By the time the day was over and the weary soldiers had lain down to rest, the Confederates were in possession of all the field, except the Landing and a bit of adjoining territory. Many Southern soldiers, in view of the gains made during the day, believed that the victory was already theirs. An equally large number of Northerners were willing to concede defeat. When night at last closed in around the hostile armies, feelings of uncertainty prevailed among the leaders on both sides. Many of them were well aware that the battle was yet to be won or lost.

The Second Day

Monday morning, April 7, at daylight, the vanquished of the previous day renewed the struggle with increased strength and restored confidence. Anxious to take the initiative, the Union armies were put in motion almost simultaneously, with Buell on the left, Lew Wallace on the extreme right, and Grant's weary troops occupying the space between. The movement began unopposed, except by small unsupported parties which were quickly forced to retreat.

The Confederates had been unable to reorganize their widely scattered forces during the night. Therefore, when the Union advance began on Monday the opposing line of battle was yet unformed. The Confederates were still back in the vicinity of the captured Union camps vainly trying to reorganize their broken commands. They did not succeed in forming a line until after the enemy had advanced beyond the Peach Orchard and the Hornets' Nest, regaining much of the territory they had lost the day before.

Young Confederate enlisted men from the Washington Artillery of New Orleans. From a photograph made prior to the Battle of Shiloh.

The Confederates, one brigade strong, were first encountered by Lew Wallace a short distance in front of his Sunday night bivouac. In a brief but spirited engagement, the Confederates were attacked in front and on the left flank by the Union division. To keep from being surrounded, they fell back almost a mile in the direction of Shiloh Church to take their place in the forming line of battle.

In the meantime, Buell moved his troops rapidly forward until they developed the Confederate line of battle west of the Peach Orchard. The Southerners boldly charged the advancing Union infantry which had moved forward so rapidly that its artillery was still far to the rear. Without artillery support, the Federals were unable to withstand the violent assault of the Confederates and were forced to make a hasty retreat. The timely arrival and effective use of two batteries of artillery permitted the Union line again to advance, only to be driven back once more by the stubborn Confederates.

The battle now raged the entire length of the field. Charge followed by countercharge moved the fitfully swaying line first toward the river and then toward the church. The advantage would seem to rest momentarily with the weary Southerners, but would soon be lost to their greatly strengthened opponent. Commands became so intermingled and confused that it was often impossible to distinguish between friend and foe. The Confederates, clad in a variety of colored uniforms, with no well-defined line and on an ever-changing front, suffered the heavier losses from the fire of their own troops.

Meanwhile, General Beauregard, at Shiloh Church, anxiously awaited the return of couriers he had dispatched to Corinth to hurry forward Gen. Earl Van Dorn's army of about 20,000 men, daily expected there from Van Buren, Ark. He had promised to make a junction with General Beauregard as soon as possible, but was delayed because he had no means of transporting his troops across the Mississippi. Unaware that Van Dorn was still in Arkansas, General Beauregard maintained his largest troop concentration in the vicinity of the church to defend the Corinth-Pittsburg Road so that reinforcements could be quickly moved onto the field. As soon as it became known that additional troops were not on the way, Beauregard realized that the road would have to be kept open as a possible line of retreat. The Union commanders were equally determined to drive the Confederates from the position. Consequently, furious fighting raged before the church long after the tempo of the battle had slackened on each flank.

Despite all efforts of the Confederates, the Union line continued slowly to advance. In desperation the Confederates made a gallant charge, first expending their ammunition and then relying on the bayonet. The charge carried the surging line through waist-deep Water Oaks Pond, beyond which the fire from the adversary became so strong that the line was brought to an abrupt halt. Taking cover at the edge of a woods, they repulsed every attempt by the Federals to advance.

Arrival of Federal reinforcements.

The first tent field hospital ever used for the treatment of the wounded on the battlefield was established at Shiloh, April 7, 1862.

By 2 p. m. General Beauregard decided it was useless to prolong the unequal struggle. Since early morning, his lines had been forced back, step by step, with heavy losses. From all parts of the field his subordinates were sending urgent requests for reinforcements, which he was unable to supply. Even his position at the church was in danger of being taken. A continuation of the battle could bring only additional disasters upon his already greatly depleted ranks. To forestall a complete rout, he ordered a rear guard with artillery support to be put in position on the ridge west of the church and instructed his corps commanders to begin withdrawing their troops. By 4 o'clock, the last of the Confederate Army, or what was left of it, had retired from the field and was leisurely making its way back to Corinth without a single Federal soldier in pursuit.

The Union armies did not attempt to harass the retreating Southern columns or attack them when they went into bivouac for the night. Instead, Grant's troops, from the privates to the highest commanders, appear to have been content to return to their recaptured camps, while the Confederates returned to their former positions in and around Corinth to recruit and reorganize.

In explanation of his inactivity Grant said: "My force was too much fatigued from two days' hard fighting and exposure in the open air to a drenching rain during the intervening night, to pursue immediately. Night closed in cloudy and with heavy rain, making roads impracticable for artillery by the next morning."

The next morning, April 8, however, Gen. Thomas J. Wood, with his division, and Sherman, with two brigades and the 4th Illinois Cavalry, went in pursuit. Toward evening they came upon the Confederate rear guard at Fallen Timbers, about 6 miles from the battlefield. The Southern cavalry, commanded by Col. Nathan Bedford Forrest, charged the Federals, putting the skirmishers to flight and throwing the Union cavalry into confusion. The Confederates, pursuing too vigorously, came suddenly upon the main body of Federal infantry and were repulsed, after Colonel Forrest had been seriously wounded in the side. Before returning to camp, the Northerners tarried long enough to bury their 15 dead, gather up their 25 wounded, and find out that they had lost 75 as prisoners. The spirited action of the Confederate rear guard at Fallen Timbers put an end to all ideas of further pursuit by the Federals.

Results of the Battle

The losses on each side at Shiloh were unusually heavy. Grant's army of 39,830 had been reinforced by 25,255 during the night between the 2 days' battle, swelling the total number of Union troops engaged to 65,085, excluding a guard detachment of 1,727 men left at Crump's Landing. Of that total number 1,754 were reported killed, 8,408 wounded, and 2,885 missing; presenting an aggregate of 13,047 casualties.

The army under Generals Johnston and Beauregard had gone into battle with 43,968 men of all arms and condition. They received no reinforcements, except 731 men of Col. Munson R. Hill's Tennessee Regiment who had reached the front unarmed and were furnished with arms and equipment picked up from the field. The Southerners lost 1,728 killed, 8,012 wounded, and 959 captured or missing, or a total of 10,699 casualties.

"Present" and "Casualties" at Shiloh

	Present for duty	Casualties			
		Killed	Wounded	Missing	Total
UNION					
Army of the Tennessee (April 6)	39,830	1,433	6,202	2,818	10,453
Reinforcements (April 7)					
Army of the Tennessee	7,337	80	399	12	491
Army of the Ohio	17,918	241	1,807	55	2,103
Total Federals engaged [1]	65,085	1,754	8,408	2,885	13,047
CONFEDERATE					
Army of the Mississippi (April 6)	43,968	1,728	8,012	959	10,699
Reinforcements (April 7)					
Hill's 47th Tennessee	731	. . .	. . .	. . .	. . .
Total Confederates engaged	44,699	1,728	8,012	959	10,699
GRAND TOTAL	109,784	3,482	16,420	3,844	23,746

[1] Does not include 1,727 troops left at Crump's Landing as rear guard.

During the first few weeks following the battle, both sides claimed a victory. The Confederates based their claim upon the facts that they had inflicted an almost complete rout on the Federals on Sunday, April 6, and that they had been able to hold a part of the field until they withdrew in good order on Monday. Furthermore, they said, the Union armies were so battered that they were unable to pursue.

Shiloh National Cemetery.

Bloody Pond.

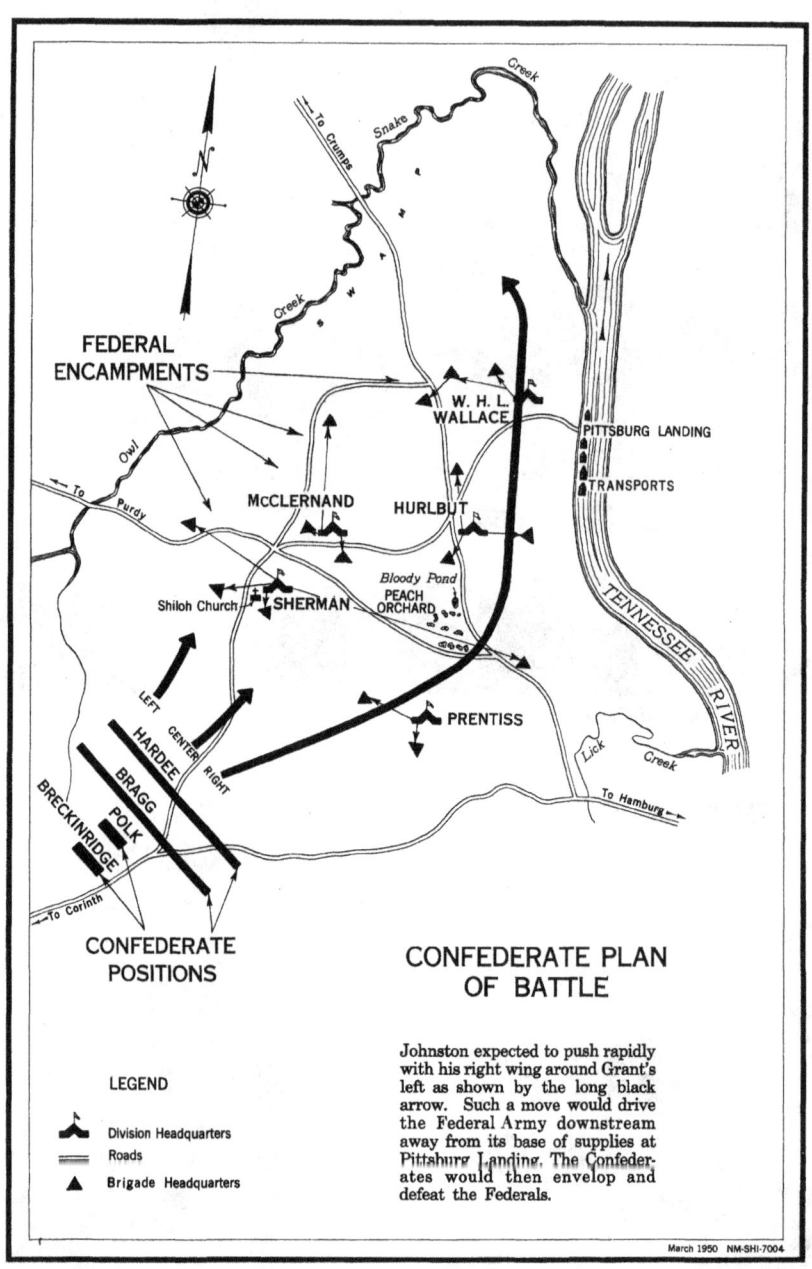

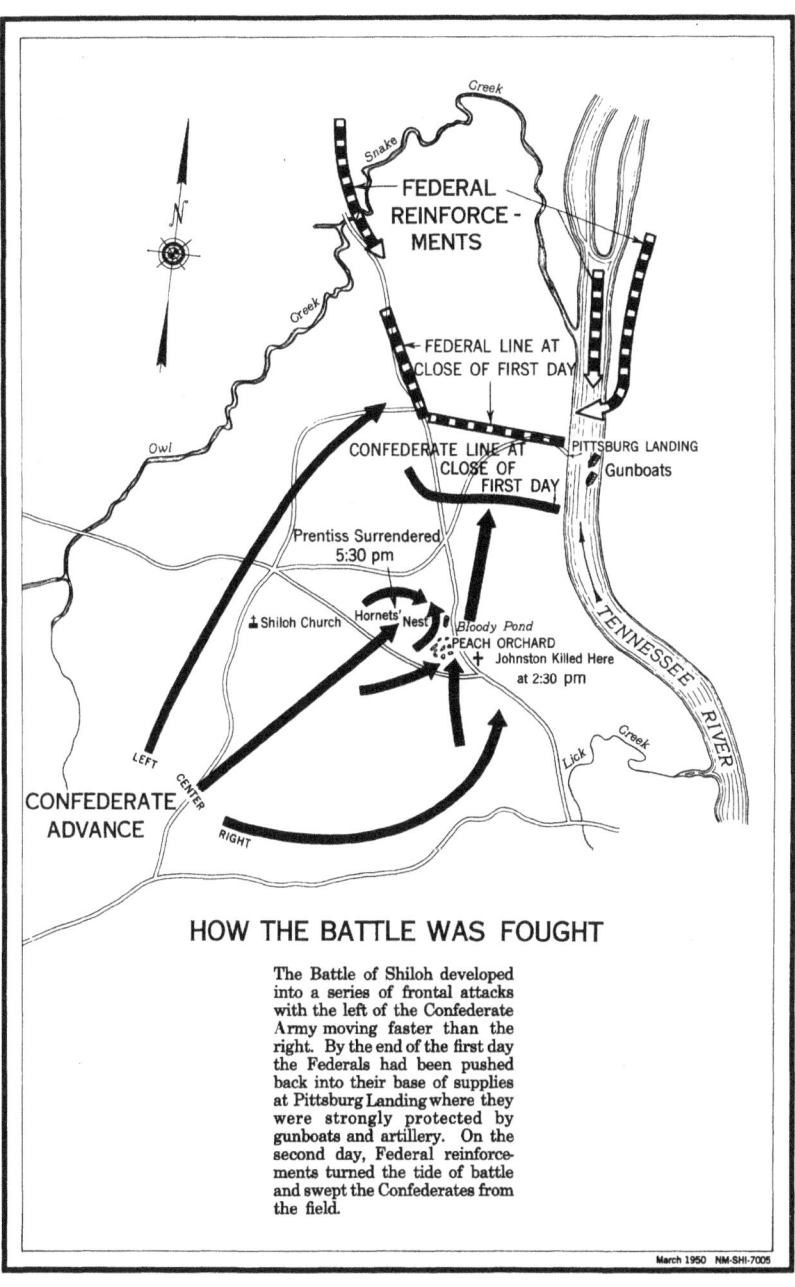

HOW THE BATTLE WAS FOUGHT

The Battle of Shiloh developed into a series of frontal attacks with the left of the Confederate Army moving faster than the right. By the end of the first day the Federals had been pushed back into their base of supplies at Pittsburg Landing where they were strongly protected by gunboats and artillery. On the second day, Federal reinforcements turned the tide of battle and swept the Confederates from the field.

March 1950 NM-SHI-7005

The Federals claimed the victory upon the grounds that on Monday evening they had recovered their encampments and had possession of the field from which the Confederates had retired, leaving behind a large number of their dead and wounded.

After the Battle of Shiloh the Confederates were compelled to withdraw southward. Corinth was abandoned to the North on May 30th, severing the railroad from Memphis to Chattanooga. By the end of June 1862, only those forts on the Mississippi River near Vicksburg remained in Southern hands. After a long siege, Vicksburg fell to the North on July 4, 1863, cutting the Confederacy in two.

Guide to the Area

For the benefit of visitors who are unable to take the guided tour, numbered markers have been placed at points of interest in the park to correspond with the following numbered sections and those shown on the guide map. For the complete tour, Nos. 1 to 17 should be followed in consecutive order.

1. IOWA STATE MONUMENT. This 75-foot monument, designed by E. F. Triebel, was erected by the State of Iowa in 1906. Surmounting the main shaft are a bronze capital, globe, and an eagle with a wingspread of 15 feet. Ascending the steps at the base of the monument is a bronze statue,

Grant's last line.

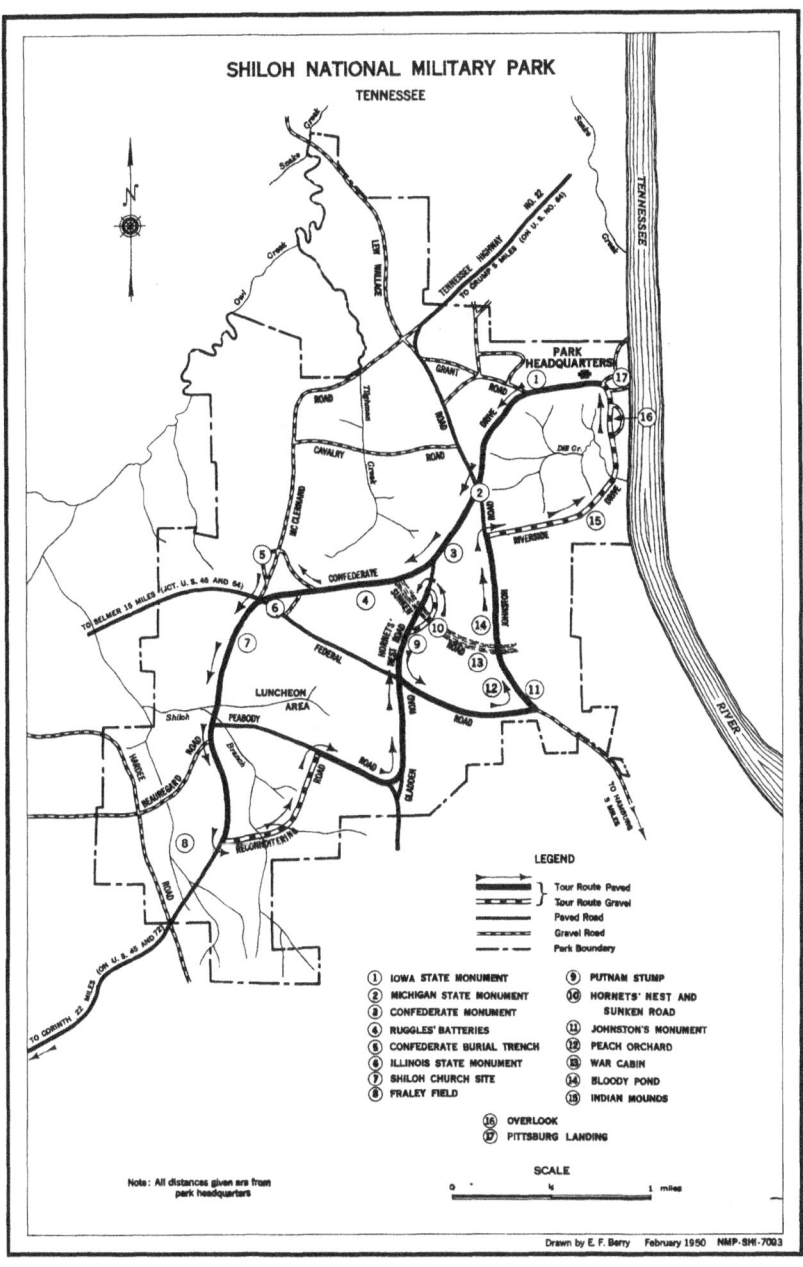

symbolic of "Fame," inscribing a tribute to the Iowa soldiers who fought in the battle. In addition to this monument, Iowa has 11 regimental monuments on the field.

The pyramid of cannon balls north of the monument marks the headquarters site of Gen. W. H. L. Wallace. When the battle opened, there were five Union divisions on the field. All of the divisional camps, except this one, were captured by the Confederates on the first day of the battle.

The siege guns southwest of the monument are the heaviest pieces used in this battle. They had an accurate range of about 2,000 yards, whereas, the ordinary cannon were effective at only about 1,100 yards. These cannon represent the last Union line, formed late Sunday afternoon, extending from the river to Snake Creek Bridge, a distance of about 2 miles.

The small earthwork beyond the siege guns is the only one thrown up on this battlefield. The emplacement was not used, however, because the Federals took the offensive early the next morning.

Confederate Monument, erected by the United Daughters of the Confederacy.

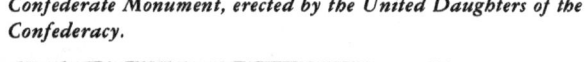

2. MICHIGAN STATE MONUMENT. Twenty-one States were represented in the Battle of Shiloh. Only 12 of those States have monuments on the battlefield. In 1918, the State of Michigan erected this memorial to her three regiments of infantry and one battery of artillery which participated in the battle. The crowning figure on the monument faces toward Corinth, Miss., the objective point of the campaign.

3. CONFEDERATE MONUMENT. This monument, designed and sculptured by Frederick C. Hibbard, was erected in 1917 by the United Daughters of the Confederacy in memory of all Southern troops who fought in the battle.

In the center of the massive pedestal is carved the bust of Gen. Albert Sidney Johnston, the Confederate commander who was killed during the afternoon of the first day.

At the extreme right, the figure in front represents the Confederate infantryman who has snatched up his flag in defiance of the Northern Army. The figure to his rear is the artilleryman who is calm as he appears to gaze through the smoke of battle.

To the left, the figure in front represents the cavalryman. His hand is spread, indicating frustration. He is eager to help, but cannot penetrate the heavy undergrowth. The figure back of the cavalryman represents the officers of the Confederate Army. He has his head bowed in submission to the order to cease firing when, it seemed, had it not been given the first day, there might have been a Confederate victory.

Duncan Field, between "Hell's Hollow" and Ruggles' Battery.

Confederate burial trench.

The central group represents a "Defeated Victory." The front figure, representing the Confederacy, is surrendering the laurel wreath of victory to Death, on the left, and Night, on the right. Death came to their commander and Night brought reinforcements to the enemy; and the battle was lost.

The panel of heads on the right represents the spirit of the first day. How hopefully and fearlessly the 11 young Confederates rushed into battle!

The panel of heads on the left represents the second day of the battle and the sorrow of the men, now reduced to 10, over the victory so nearly won and so unexpectedly lost.

South of the monument, just inside the woods, is the spot where Union General Prentiss surrendered, with over 2,200 troops, at 5:30 p. m., on the first day.

4. RUGGLES' BATTERIES. The line of guns on the left represents Ruggles' Confederate concentration of 62 cannon. This was the longest line of artillery ever formed in an American battle up to that time. Aided by these cannon, the Confederates succeeded in driving back the Union flanks and in capturing over 2,200 troops near the center of the Hornets' Nest.

5. CONFEDERATE BURIAL TRENCH. All of the Confederate dead are buried on the battlefield in five large trenches. In this, the largest, there are, reportedly, 721 bodies, stacked seven deep.

New Shiloh Church, stands on the site of the original church.

The day after the battle, General Beauregard dispatched a message to General Grant asking for permission to send a mounted party to the battlefield to bury his dead. In answer, Grant said: "Owing to the warmth of the weather I deemed it advisable to have all the dead of both parties buried immediately . . . now it is accomplished."

The Confederates and Federals were buried alike in separate trenches on the field. Four years after the battle the Union dead were removed to the newly established national cemetery. The Confederates still rest in the trenches where they were buried by the Federal troops.

6. ILLINOIS STATE MONUMENT. This monument, sculptured by Richard W. Bock, was dedicated in 1904 to all Illinois troops who participated in the battle of Shiloh.

The crowning figure, designed to represent the State of Illinois, holds a book in her left hand containing a record of her sons' achievements on this field. In her right hand is a sheathed sword. The scabbard is held with a firm grasp as if in readiness for release of the blade and a renewal of the battle should the occasion arise. Her gaze is bent watchfully toward enemy territory to the south.

7. SHILOH CHURCH SITE. The original "Shiloh Meeting House"—a one-room log structure with rude handmade furnishings—was built by the Southern Methodists about 1853, 9 years after the church had split over the slavery issue.

When the Union Army moved upon the field, General Sherman encamped his division along the ridge on either side of the church. It was along this same ridge that he formed his first line of battle on the morning of April 6, 1862, and where he was first attacked by the Confederates. He succeeded in holding the ridge for about 2 hours before he was forced to withdraw.

As soon as Sherman withdrew, General Beauregard established his headquarters at the church. He held the position until the Confederates began their retreat on the second day.

The church was reportedly torn down by the Union troops and the logs used to build bridges when the movement upon Corinth began.

The present structure, completed in 1949, stands on the site of the original church.

8. FRALEY FIELD. About 3 a. m. on Sunday, April 6, a reconnoitering party was sent out from Prentiss' division to explore a small wagon trail to the front. The party, under Major Powell, advanced past Seay Field, crossed the main Corinth Road, and encountered the Confederate cavalry videttes at the corner of Wood and Fraley Fields at 4:55 a. m. There followed an engagement with the pickets, commanded by Major Hardcastle, from Wood's brigade of Hardee's corps.

About 6:30 a. m., the Confederate advance began. The reconnoitering party fell back slowly, making a stand at the corner of Seay Field. By 7:30 a. m., the Confederate line had advanced to within half a mile of Prentiss' camps.

9. PUTNAM STUMP. Pvt. John D. Putnam, Company F, 14th Wisconsin Volunteer Infantry, was killed on Monday, April 7, during a charge against a Confederate battery. He was buried where he fell, at the foot of a young oak tree.

Thomas Stone, one of the burying party, suggested that his name be carved into the tree sufficiently low so that in case the tree were cut down the name would remain.

When the national cemetery was established, Putnam's body was removed to it. Because of the precautions of his comrades in 1862, his is one of the few graves marked with full name, company, and regiment.

In 1901, the Wisconsin Shiloh Monument Commission visited the field to select a site for the State monument. They found that the tree had been chopped down, but that the stump remained with the name of Putnam still legible. The Wisconsin Commissioners chose this spot because of its absolute correctness as to the position of the 14th Regiment. They decided to reproduce the stump in granite and to place it on the exact spot where the original had stood. This unusual monument to a private was placed in position April 7, 1906.

Putnam Stump.

10. HORNETS' NEST AND SUNKEN ROAD. The Confederate soldiers named this area "Hornets' Nest" because of the stinging shot and shell they had to face here. Parts of three Federal divisions were intrenched in this old sunken road, protected by a heavy rail fence and dense undergrowth.

General Ruggles, after having witnessed 11 unsuccessful attacks against the position, formed a line of artillery consisting of 62 pieces and concentrated its fire upon the Federal line. With the aid of these cannon, the Confederates were able to form a circle around the Sunken Road, surrounding and capturing General Prentiss, with more than 2,200 troops, at 5:30 p. m.

Within this area are the Arkansas, Minnesota, and Wisconsin State Monuments.

11. JOHNSTON'S MONUMENT. On the afternoon of April 6, General Johnston ordered his reserves to go into action and advance on the right flank in an attempt to drive a wedge between the Federal troops and their base of supplies at Pittsburg Landing. He also hoped to make it impossible for reinforcements to come to Grant's assistance from across the river. While personally directing his reserves, he was struck in the right leg by a Minié ball which cut the large artery.

Johnston's Mortuary Monument.

At the time General Johnston was struck, he was sitting on his horse, "Fire-eater," underneath the large oak tree now enclosed by an iron fence. He was taken to the ravine about 100 yards south of this monument. There, beneath the tree now protected by another iron fence, he died from loss of blood, a few minutes later.

Four other mortuary monuments are located in the park, marking the spots where Generals Gladden and W. H. L. Wallace and Colonels Peabody and Raith fell in action.

12. PEACH ORCHARD. At the time of the battle, the Peach Orchard was in full bloom. It was here that some of the hardest fighting of the first day took place. While the fighting raged across the orchard, bullets were cutting the blossoms from the trees so thick and fast that the air appeared to be filled with falling snow.

13. WAR CABIN. This cabin formerly stood in Perry Field on the Federal right and in the immediate front of the last Union line established on Sunday afternoon, the first day of the battle. The battle-scarred logs reveal that it stood in the midst of heavy fighting. Of the many cabins on the field at the time of the battle, this is the only survivor.

The cabin was moved to the present location, a few weeks after the battle, to replace one that was burned during the engagement.

14. BLOODY POND. This shallow pool of water was in the path of the retreating Federal Army as it was pushed back toward the river on Sunday. Being the only water in the immediate vicinity, the wounded from both sides crawled here to quench their thirst and bathe their wounds. So many bled in and around the pond that the water is said to have become stained the color of blood.

15. INDIAN MOUNDS. There are about 30 mounds in this area, 7 of which are large, ranging in height from 5 to 15 feet. With one exception, all are flat-topped platform mounds. The one having a different form is an oval-shaped burial mound.

The mounds were excavated in 1934 under the direction of the Smithsonian Institution. Quantities of broken pottery, bone implements, stone tools, and weapons were removed. Twelve skeletons were found in the oval burial mound.

The effigy pipe, now on display at park headquarters, was removed from the burial mound in 1899 under the direction of the Park Commission.

16. OVERLOOK. This 100-foot bluff affords the best view of the Tennessee River and the adjoining country. From this point one can see the east bank of the river where the advance of General Buell's army, following its march from Savannah, Tenn., embarked to cross to the battlefield late Sunday afternoon.

War cabin.

Red stone effigy pipe found in one of the burial mounds.

Down the river, to the north, one can see Savannah where General Grant had his headquarters. On clear days, Pickwick Dam may be seen up the river, to the south.

17. PITTSBURG LANDING. Even before the Battle of Shiloh, this was an important landing. Merchants of Corinth, Purdy, and the adjacent country received most of their merchandise from boats which tied up at this point. When the boats went back downstream, they were laden with passengers, cotton, and produce which had been transported to the Landing over the roads which converged here.

When the Union armies began preparations for the move against Corinth, Pittsburg Landing was selected as the concentration point because of its good camp sites and the good roads which led to the Confederate stronghold. The Army of the Tennessee, with the exception of Lew Wallace's 3d Division, debarked at Pittsburg Landing. General Buell's army, brought to Grant's aid under the stress of battle, arrived at the field on such a large number of transports that the Landing would not accommodate them. Consequently, all of the riverbank within the Union lines was used as a boat landing.

Excursion boat departing from Pittsburg Landing.

Because of the importance of the Landing, the engagement was called "Battle of Pittsburg Landing" in most Northern newspapers and reports. The Southern name "Battle of Shiloh" is now almost universally accepted.

National Cemetery

Shiloh National Cemetery was established in 1866 and embraces an area of 10.2 acres. In the cemetery are interred 3,695 bodies, two-thirds of whom are unidentified. Besides the Union soldiers killed in the Battle of Shiloh, the cemetery holds many of the dead from nearby battlefields. In addition, a number of those who served in the Spanish-American War, both World Wars, and one from the Revolutionary War are buried here. Only two Confederates are buried in the cemetery. Both died while being held as prisoners of war.

The Wisconsin Color Guard Memorial is located at the east end of the cemetery on the bluff overlooking the Tennessee River. Another interesting feature of the cemetery is the pyramid of 32-pounder cannon erected by the United States Government to mark the site of the tree used by General Grant as headquarters on the night of April 6.

How to Reach the Park

Shiloh National Military Park is situated on the west bank of the Tennessee River at the intersection of State Highways Nos. 22 and 142. It is 13 miles east of U. S. No. 45, and 5 miles south of U. S. No. 64.

Graves of six Wisconsin color bearers, overlooking Tennessee River. In Shiloh National Cemetery.

Administration

Shiloh National Military Park is administered by the National Park Service of the United States Department of the Interior. A superintendent, whose address is Pittsburg Landing, Tenn., is in immediate charge.

The Park and Related Areas

Shiloh National Military Park, containing about 3,730 acres of Federal land, was established by act of Congress in 1894. At the time of its establishment only Chickamauga and Chattanooga National Military Park, Ga.-Tenn., had been dedicated in memory of the western campaigns of the War Between the States. In subsequent years other national military parks dealing with the Civil War in the West have been established. Those most closely related to Shiloh are Vicksburg National Military Park, Miss., and Stones River and Fort Donelson National Military Parks, Tenn.

Visitor Facilities

An exhibit room and library are located in the administration building, situated near Pittsburg Landing. They may be visited by the public every day from 8 a. m. to 4:30 p. m. Here are to be found interesting relics, books, and maps relating to the Battle of Shiloh and the Civil War. Free literature concerning this area may also be secured at park headquarters. Orientation and historical talks are given daily by members of the park staff. Free guide service is usually available. Special service is provided for groups and organizations if arrangements are made in advance with the superintendent.

Shiloh Inspires Writers

For the first two or three decades following the Battle of Shiloh many literary men, following the dictates of popular demand, based their compositions, both prose and poetry, upon events of that bloody battle. Since Shiloh was significant for the bravery of the young untrained men of the North and South alike, writers frequently wrote about the young

Administration building.

"The Drummer Boy of Shiloh," written in 1862, was one of more than 300 songs published by Will S. Hays.

and otherwise undistinguished soldiers rather than the time-worn theme of the brave and gallant leaders. The drummer boy, often a mere lad who had run away from home to seek adventure in the ranks, became the subject of some of the most popular literature of the day. Many of these productions were based upon incidents which actually happened during the engagement, but those destined to become most famous were drawn largely from the imaginative minds of the authors.

Samuel J. Muscroft's play *The Drummer Boy of Shiloh,* written in 1870, was apparently based upon "what might have been" rather than facts.

The play—a pleasing mixture of drama, pathos, and comedy—was staged in cities and towns all over the Northern States for almost 40 years. It was ordinarily staged as a home-town production rather than by professional actors and actresses—a factor which tended to increase its popularity. In fact, contemporary accounts say that the play was second in popularity only to *Uncle Tom's Cabin.*

Numerous poems about Shiloh were of immediate, if not lasting, popularity. Herman Melville, author of *Moby Dick* and *Typee,* attracted by the multitude of inviting subjects presented by the Civil War, turned

to Shiloh for inspiration. "Shiloh," published 4 years after the battle, is one of his most famous poems of the War Between the States era.

"The Men of the West" by Richard Coe; "Our Boys who Fell at Shiloh" and "General Albert Sidney Johnston" by H. Pleasants McDaniel; and "The Old Sergeant" by Forceythe Willson are typical examples of the trend in poetry immediately following Shiloh.

Song writers of the period also looked to Shiloh for the themes of their melodies. The most successful endeavor in this field was made by Will S. Hays in "The Drummer Boy of Shiloh." Like the play by that name, the song is undoubtedly based upon fancy rather than facts. The title was chosen because of its certain musical quality and not because of its connection with any incident of the engagement. Hays, a correspondent of the *Louisville Democrat,* wrote the song in 1862 while the story of the battle was still news rather than history. It is not known whether he was at the battle of Shiloh or whether his sympathies were with the North or the South. However, his song immediately became famous throughout the country and remained popular for a number of years.

The song and the play, "The Drummer Boy of Shiloh," may possibly be credited with the creation, or at least the perpetuation, of the popular legend about "The Drummer Boy of Shiloh." After the publication of these works several claimants to the title came to the fore. Needless to say, these men had not been killed at the battle, but each maintained that his presence at the engagement as a youthful drummer had inspired the authors. From time to time, as years passed, newspapers in widely scattered sections of the country announced "The Drummer Boy of

Shiloh Dies." A recent study by Ray H. Mattison, former historian at Shiloh National Military Park, proved that many of the claimants were ineligible for the designation. In the final analysis, John Clem, "The Drummer Boy of Chickamauga," was found to have the strongest claim to the Shiloh title.

THE DRUMMER BOY OF SHILOH

"Look down upon the battlefield,
Oh Thou, Our Heavenly Friend,
Have mercy on our sinful souls."
The soldiers cried, "Amen."
There gathered 'round a little group,
Each brave man knelt and cried.
They listened to the drummer boy,
Who prayed before he died.

"Oh, Mother," said the dying boy,
"Look down from heaven on me.
Receive me to thy fond embrace,
Oh, take me home to thee.
I've loved my country as my God.
To serve them both I've tried!"
He smiled, shook hands—death seized the boy,
Who prayed before he died.

Each soldier wept then like a child.
Stout hearts were they and brave.
They wrapped him in his country's flag
And laid him in the grave.
They placed by him the Bible,
A rededicated guide
To those that mourn the drummer boy
Who prayed before he died.

Ye angels 'round the throne of grace,
Look down upon the braves,
Who fought and died on Shiloh's plain,
Now slumbering in their graves.
How many homes made desolate,
How many hearts have sighed.
How many like that drummer boy,
Who prayed before he died.

—WILL S. HAYS.

The years intervening between the Battle of Shiloh and the present have softened the harshness of the engagement and wrapped it in a shroud of sentimental romanticism. Most twentieth-century writers are content to view the battle from that perspective. Occasionally a realist, such as Shelby Foote in his historical novel, "Shiloh," penetrates the rosy glow and brings forth interesting and all-but-forgotten facts. Dr. Merrick F. McCarthy, another twentieth-century writer, presents an accurate and vivid picture of the battle in the following poem:

FOUR VOICES FROM SHILOH*

Stern Johnston came in April from the South
To spread the Shiloh fields with threatening Gray!
Hard Sherman set his unrelenting mouth,
And Grant knew not the season or the day,
Though spring had come! A turmoil held the Land
In vast confusion, out of which these three
Came on, with purpose clear, with sword in hand,
To meet on Shiloh Field their destiny!

Where their lines struck live now but squirrel and bird!
Calm April has her way with flower and tree,—
But there are lasting voices to be heard
At Pittsburg Landing on the Tennessee!

FIRST VOICE
(That of a young man from the North)

If Grant and Sherman push on through,
We'll cut the Southern States in two!
It's not a question of white or black,—
But when States leave, we'll bring them back!
They talk and talk in Washington,
While in the South they're training men!
We had 'em whipped at Donelson,—
But now they're ready to fight again!

When the brood mare foals, I'll be away,—
I always spaded the garden in spring!
And what of the oats, the wheat and the hay?
Who will shock as the reapers swing?
Or mend the roads in thicket and copse,
Or boil the syrup from maple drops?

*Copyright by author.

*Timber to fell, fires to make,—
Ice to cut on the frozen lake!
I wonder if Dad will be able to plow,—
And whether Mother is living now?*

*Why do we stay on Shiloh hill,
With our backs to the muddy river;
With Rebels to fight and Rebels to kill,
Why camp in the woods and shiver?
We drilled with Sherman in Ohio,
And now by the Tennessee!
Where do the Southern pickets go
That fire on you and me?
I reckon to Corinth to drill in the mud,—
But we have drilled a few
Who stained the Michie hill with blood
To remember me and you!*

SECOND VOICE
(That of a young Southern man)

*Hang all Yanks to the end of a limb!
One of us equals ten of him!
What's a Southern man to do
But load his rifle and see this through?
The Yankee Buell is miles away,
While Sherman here on Shiloh creek,
Has no entrenchments, so they say!
Let's hit the Yanks while they are weak!
But winter is here and times are hard,—
I wonder who'll slaughter and render the lard
With me in Corinth? Who'll tend the mill,
With corn on hand and orders to fill?
Dragging guns through water and mud,
With cotton to plant and rice to flood!
The Army's taken our horses and mules
And the children walk to the parish schools!
General Johnston's almighty slow
Gettin' this army ready to go!*

*And who in hell made the Corinth road?
Horse to leather, man to rope,—
Slither, stagger with the load,—
Through rain, the mud and darkness grope!
Timber the ruts where the freshets run,—*

> *Dam off the floods; move up, move on,—*
> *Live or die, but every gun*
> *Must reach the ridge with its caisson!*
> *Cover your powder from the wet;*
> *Keep hammers clean and barrels dry,—*
> *Wipe your pistol and bayonet!*
> *Tomorrow watch the Yankees die!*

THIRD VOICE
(That of an old army sergeant)

> *Privates sleep where the rain pours down!*
> *Generals have a bed in town!*
> *Hayfoot, strawfoot never knows*
> *Whether his gun is loaded or not!*
> *Load again and if she blows . . .*
> *Dead and buried, and soon forgot!*

(A ringing rifle volley is heard)

> *Volley fire! That's what you hear!*
> *And that means more than a picket brush!*
> *Turn your head away from the rear*
> *And set yourself for their first rush!*
> *(Load your guns, if you know how,*
> *With your fingers stiff with fright!*
> *Northern boys from yard and mow,*
> *Southern boys from field and plow,*
> *God forbid, your time is now!)*
> *Dress your line! The guide is right!*

(The sounds of battle rise to a crescendo then fade to the silence of the woods)

FOURTH VOICE
(That of an elderly farmer)

> *Pray God they never march again*
> *Across my farm, tearing the land to bits,—*
> *Wheeling their guns and leaving broken men*
> *Blasted and burned wherever shell-fire hits!*
> *I have the papers now about the fight*
> *That rolled across my orchard, ridge and hill!*
> *Half of the truth is all they dare to write*
> *About what happens when men fight to kill!*

Now this: "Cleburne advanced across the stream"!
Advanced! He met a line that crashed and flamed
Not loud enough to cover up the scream,
As those in front fell over dead and maimed!
Over the fallen who still shrieked and cried,
The Mississippi troops moved in the flash
Of Sherman's powder, burning as they died,
Meeting the fire with stab and saber slash!

"Sherman fell back"! They ran from tree to tree
Along the greening ridge, now blue with smoke,
Where struggling wounded staggered desperately,
Holding torn arms or legs that bent and broke!
Fell slowly back through burning oak and beech,
Carrying an officer shot through the chest!
Behind my orchard bright with blooming peach,
"Prentiss took line across the Hornets' Nest"!

Out of the "Sunken Road" men rose to fire
Into the faces of advancing men
Who found the flaming leaves a funeral pyre,—
While those who lived rallied and charged again!
Around my little pond they clubbed and fired
Until the banks were beaten into mud,
Where lay the crying wounded, trapped and mired,
Bleeding until the water stained with blood!

"Then Ruggles massing his artillery
Opened his fire upon the Union line,"
Shaking the earth with blazing battery
That razed the trees, the thickets and the vine!
Men and my fence dissolved in splintering sound
To red-stained rubble! Then "General Wallace fell,"—
And when his men saw him knocked to the ground,
The center broke, and both the wings as well!

Pushed to the river bank, for one last stand,
Artillery and infantry stood side by side,
Guarding the only place where boats might land!
"Hold now"! Or drown in the Confederate tide!
Then on this wild confusion, darkness came,
And with the darkness, rain and piercing chill,
Lit only by the sudden, thundering flame,
A Union gunboats fired across the hill . . .

*All night they carried wounded back to town,—
By barge and boat,—and some they put to knife
In that small shack, near where the steps go down,
With screaming I'll remember all my life!
Their General Grant just couldn't stand the sound
The wounded made! He sat out by a tree
Under a little tent and nearly drowned
In rain; sitting as close as you to me!*

*Fresh Yankee troops crossed over through the night,—
Buell's troops, come down from Nashville way!
Grant sent them in and started up the fight
As soon as there was light, come break of day!
Then hell broke loose again across my farm,—
More frightened, screaming men came running back,
Coughing and bloody,—broke in leg or arm,—
And some with powder burns, completely black!*

*By afternoon, they said it was a rout,—
But no one followed far, that I could see!
While Beauregard got his Confederates out,
The Yankees seemed content to let them be!
And when they told me General Johnston died
In my ravine, I thought: "The South is dead"!
And so thought those who took that Corinth ride
With their dead general in a wagon-bed!*

*And I thought too: this farm is dead to me!
I'll never cross my orchard lot again
But I'll remember how it looked to see
My pasture spread with fallen, silent men!
But there is fruit again; the grass is high,—
I guess by fall I'll have my fences set!
I've got some hay down, lying cut to dry,—
And hard work helps a man who must forget!*

*And I keep thinking that it may not be
The South has met her end! This may begin
A time when men no longer feel so free
To say to other men: you live in sin
For which there's need to cure you with a gun!
It could be here was born a brotherhood,—
That from this waste and ruin we have won
A hope for us as yet not understood!*

I wonder too about this Lincoln man!
He must have feelings just as you and I!
He must have thought when all this fight began:
O God Almighty, now more men must die!
He's uglier than sin, but maybe he
Will keep his will above the sound of guns
And not turn arrogant in victory,
Remembering how the South, too, lost her sons!

I wept and prayed while I threw in the dead
Like lumps of soil: "O God of all Creation,—
Let it not be in vain our sons have bled!
In your Son's name,
     MAKE US AGAIN A NATION!"*

DSI's New Releases:
Civil War Battlefield Guides

ISBN	Title	Page Count	Price
1582187770	Manassas (Bull Run)	56	$8.95
1582187789	Chickamauga and Chattanooga Battlefields	72	$8.95
1582187800	Gettysburg National Military Park	60	$8.95
1582187819	Shiloh National Military Park, Tennessee	58	$8.95
1582187827	Antietam National Battlefield Site, Maryland	72	$8.95
1582187835	Petersburg National Military Park, Virginia	68	$8.95
1582187843	Fort Sumter National Monument, South Carolina	56	$8.95

To order visit:
www.PDFLibrary.com

www.ingramcontent.com/pod-product-compliance
Lightning Source LLC
Chambersburg PA
CBHW031432040426
42444CB00006B/776